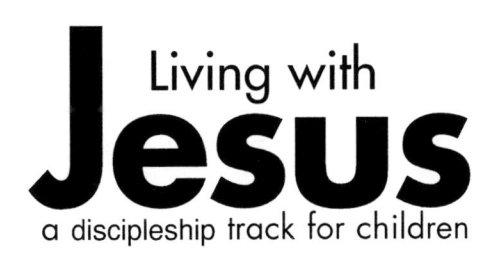

Living with Jesus
a discipleship track for children

Strongholds
Introducing children to strongholds - the soul and freedom

Daphne Kirk

G2g
Generation 2 generation

First published in 1999 by
KEVIN MAYHEW LTD
Buxhall, Stowmarket, Suffolk IP14 3DJ

Designed by Angela Palfrey
Edited by Helen Elliot

2nd printing in 2004 by
Daphne Kirk

© 1999 Daphne Kirk

The right of Daphne Kirk to be identified as the author of this work has been asserted by her in accordance with the Copyright, Designs and Patents Act 1988.

No part of this publication may be reproduced, stored in a retrieval system, or transmitted, in any form or by any means, electronic, mechanical, photocopying, recording or otherwise, without the prior written permission of the publisher.

All rights reserved.

Scripture references are taken from the Holy Bible, New International Version, unless otherwise stated. Copyright © 1973, 1978, 1984, by International Bible Society. Used by permission of Hodder & Stoughton Limited.

0 1 2 3 4 5 6 7 8 9

ISBN 1 84003 338 X
Catalogue No 1500258

Printed and bound in the United States of America

Contact Daphne Kirk by email via her website:
www.gnation2gnation.com

Introduction

Living with Jesus is a tool for discipleship. It can be used in a variety of settings, but perhaps the most effective will be in the context of child and parent.

The adult is named a 'special friend' in the material so this can be applied to a parent or responsible adult.

The following guidelines will help you to achieve the best from the time spent with your child. Meet with one child at a time; each child is different!

1. Anticipate that you will change and grow with the child; apply the material to yourself also.

2. Try to have one session a week with your child (values cannot be changed every day!).

3. *Living With Jesus* aims to stimulate sharing and deepen relationships, so take your time together in a relaxed, quiet environment.

4. The material is not designed to answer questions, but to reveal issues that need to be talked through.

5. If you are not the parent, always gain the permission of the parent. Show them the material. Ask if they would like to join you as you meet with the child. Stay in a place where you can be seen and heard by others, i.e. not behind closed doors.

6. Remember that honest answers are 'right' answers.

7. If you are unsure how to react, or unsure of an answer, it is all right to tell the child that you will talk about it again the next time you meet, and take some time to pray or ask for help.

8. Find creative ways to learn the memory verse, i.e. put actions to it, draw a picture of it, fill in words, make them into plaques, etc.

Remember that this is one of the most important times with your child. You have all the wisdom and anointing of the Holy Spirit available to you. Enjoy your time…have fun and expect Jesus to be at the centre!

*To Megan and Harry
and the next generation*

Contents

Session 1: **The soul**   7

Session 2: **Having a stronghold**   13

Session 3: **Rejoicing souls**   19

Session 4: **The enemy**   27

Session 5: **Down with strongholds!**   33

Session 6: **Looking back and going on**   39

Strongholds

My name is: _____

My friend is: _____

My church is: _____
_____
_____

We will meet on: _____
_____

My address is: _____
_____
_____
_____
_____

1
The soul

The soul

Today I want to talk to you about a part of you called the

SOUL

Have you ever heard anyone talking about the soul? Yes/No

I'll explain it to you, then you will understand when you hear it again.

Your body has different parts –
hands, legs, ears, arms, feet.

> Your **soul** has different parts . . .
>
> your **mind** – where you do your thinking;
>
> your **will** – where you choose;
>
> your **emotions** – where you feel things like happiness, sadness, excitement, fear.

So

I **think** in my *mind*

I **feel** with my emotions

I **choose** with my will

Q Can you fill in the spaces?

My soul

My
_ _ _ _
is where I
THINK

My
_ _ _ _
is where I
CHOOSE

My
_ _ _ _ _ _ _
are where I
FEEL

If you put them all together it makes your **SOUL**.

My MIND
is where I
_ _ _ _ _

My WILL
is where I
_ _ _ _ _ _

My EMOTIONS
are where I
_ _ _ _

THIS IS MY SOUL

So –

I **THINK** about Jesus in my _____

I **CHOOSE** to follow Him in my _____

I **FEEL** His joy in my _____

Then my **SOUL** is praising Jesus.

9

Read Psalm 146:1

Praise the Lord, O my _ _ _ _

THINK about Jesus

CHOOSE to follow Him

and **FEEL** Him with you.

Then you can say, like Mary in Luke 1:46

'**My soul** _ _ _ _ _ _ _ _ _ (that means *praises*) **the Lord.**'

My SOUL PRAISES THE LORD

You could colour this.

Memory Verse

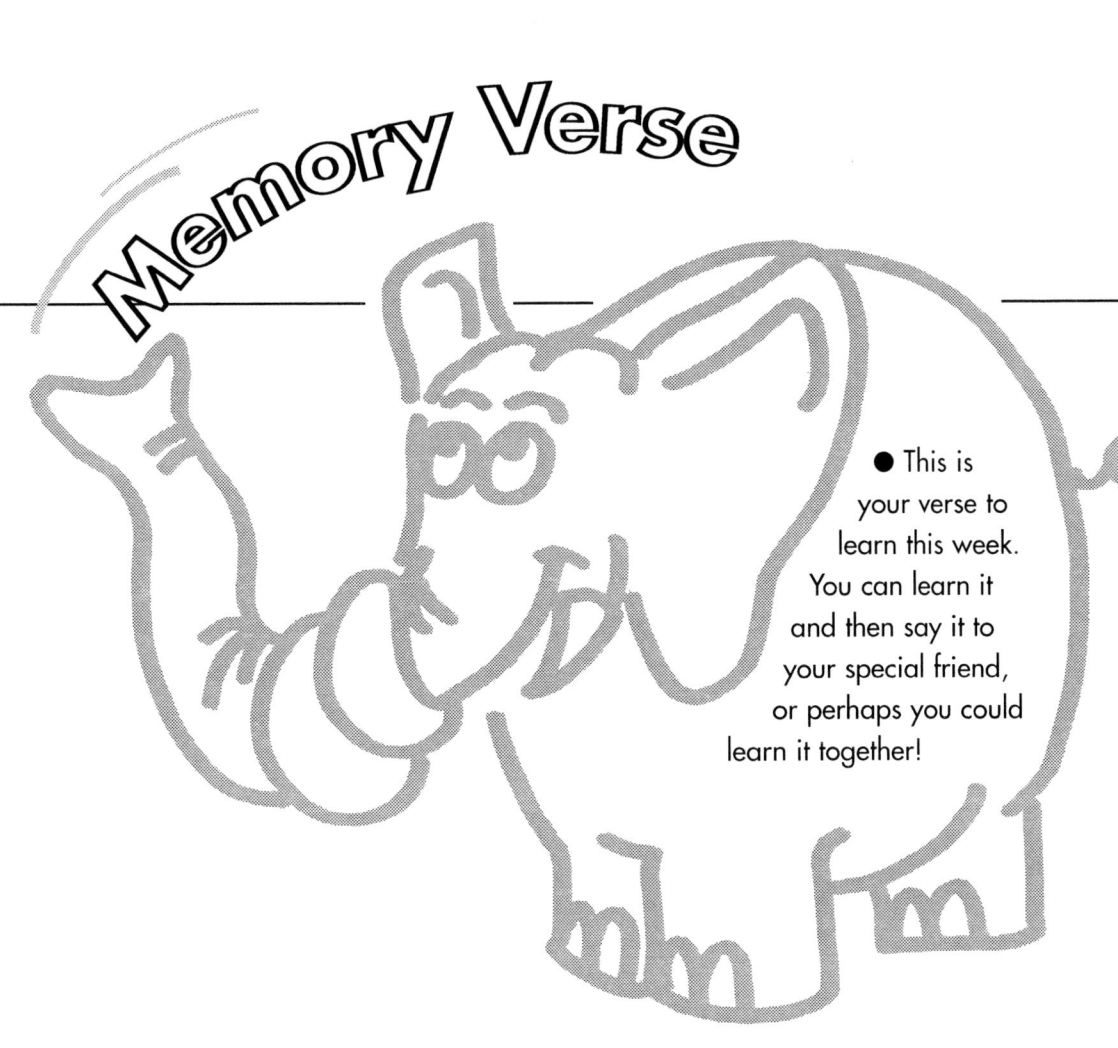

● This is your verse to learn this week. You can learn it and then say it to your special friend, or perhaps you could learn it together!

Praise the Lord,
O my soul.
I will praise the Lord
all my life.
I will sing praise to my God
as long as I live.

Psalm 146:1, 2

More sharing together

1. Ask your special friend about a time when they had to <u>choose</u> to do something that they found quite difficult (using their <u>will</u>).

2. Tell your special friend about a time when you were happy and a time when you were sad (your <u>emotions</u>).

3. Share with each other something you <u>think</u> about very often (your <u>minds</u>).

2

Having a stronghold

Having a stronghold

In the kingdom controlled by Satan sin doesn't matter. You can walk about and not worry about sins.

Satan's kingdom

Stealing

Cheating

Bad friendships

Watching horrible TV programmes

Using money wrongly

When the Kingdom of God begins to invade Satan's kingdom, there is a

WAR

These things try to stop the Kingdom of God – they put up a fight.

They become **STRONGHOLDS.**

They **HOLD ON STRONGLY TO SATAN'S LAND.**

THEY HOLD ON SO STRONGLY

that nothing you do seems to be able to get them out of your life.

BUT

is there anything that has such a stronghold that it can beat

Jesus?

NO!

2 Corinthians 10:4
says that we have weapons and that the weapons we fight
with are not like the ones we have in the world, but they have

God's power to _ _ _ _ _ _ _ _ strongholds

(look right at the end of the verse)

'Demolish' means to get rid of completely, so there is nothing left at all. That is what can happen to a stronghold when God's power is released against it!

You could learn to say this rap together loudly and strongly!

**Whatever has a stronghold,
it must go, go, go!
Whatever holds me strongly,
it must GO!**

**When Jesus goes to war,
then Satan can be sure,
that whatever holds on strongly,
it must GO!**

Memory Verse

● This is your verse to learn this week. You can learn it and then say it to your special friend, or perhaps you could learn it together!

The weapons we fight with
are not the weapons
of the world . . .
they have divine power
to demolish strongholds.

2 Corinthians 10:4

More sharing together

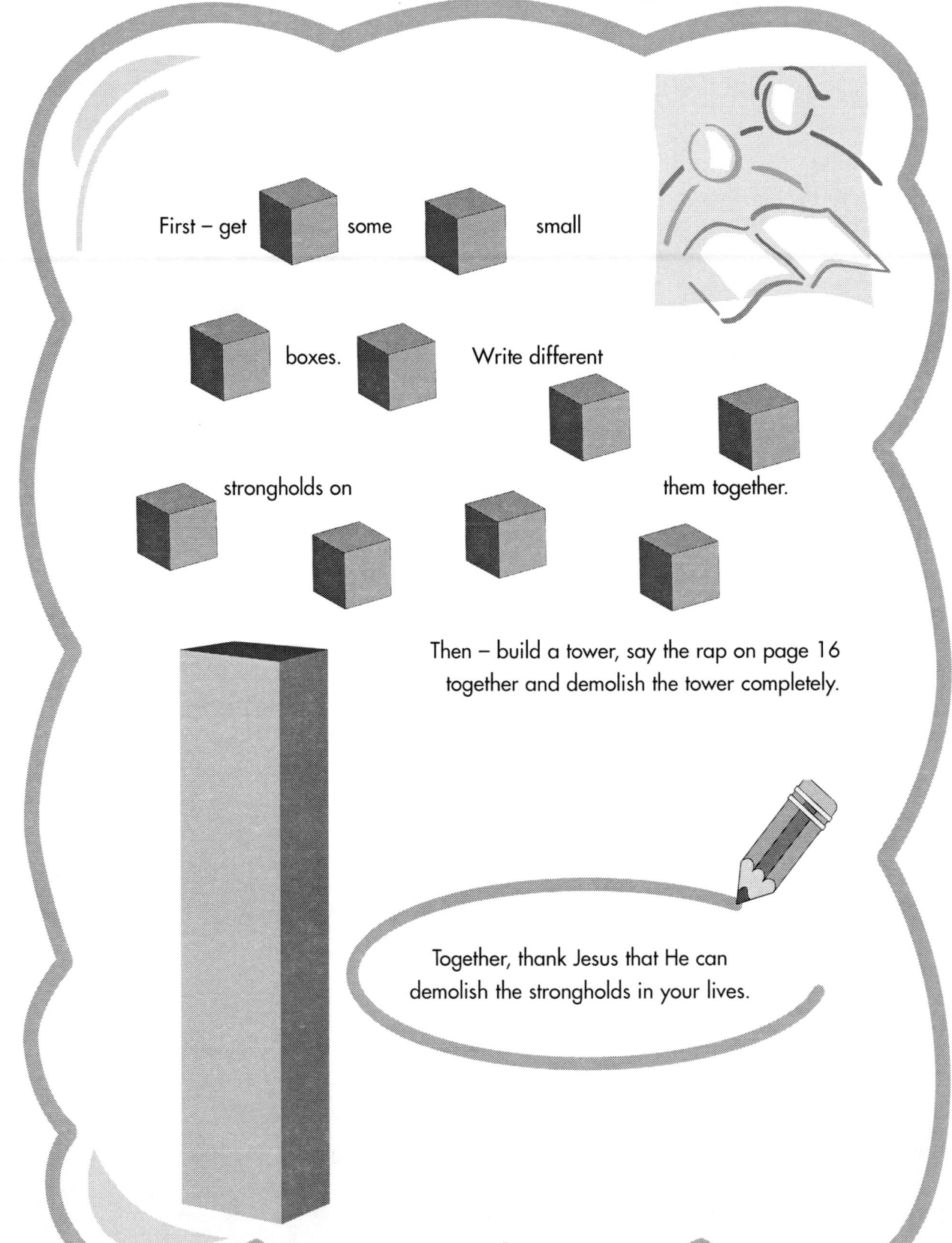

First – get some small boxes. Write different strongholds on them together.

Then – build a tower, say the rap on page 16 together and demolish the tower completely.

Together, thank Jesus that He can demolish the strongholds in your lives.

18

3
Rejoicing souls

Rejoicing souls

We have talked about your soul and about strongholds. Let's see what happens when we put these two things together.
But first read back over the pages you have already been through.

Have you read them?   Yes/No

SOUL

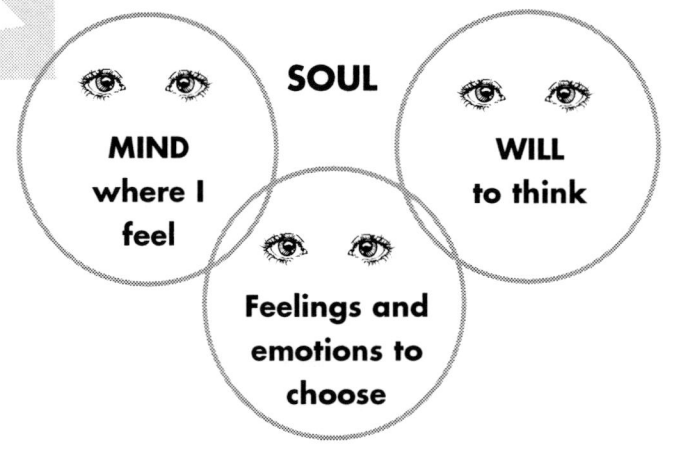

MIND
where I feel

WILL
to think

Feelings and emotions to choose

Can you find the mistakes in these drawings?
Put a circle round every mistake you can find.

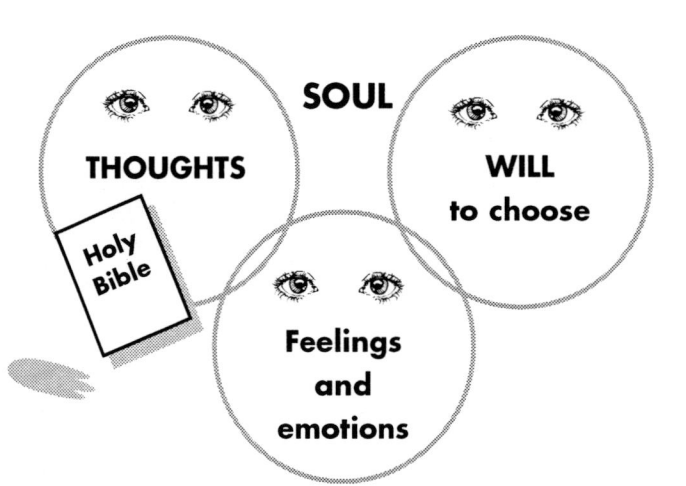

SOUL

THOUGHTS

Holy Bible

WILL
to choose

Feelings and emotions

You can colour the pictures of the soul today.
This time the soul has pretend eyes!

In this picture, the mind has the Word of God in it. So the mind is thinking about the Word of God,
the will is choosing what to do by looking at the Word of God,
and the emotions are feeling as Jesus wants them to feel.

All of the soul –
> **the mind (thinking)**
> **the will (choosing)**
> **the emotions (feeling)**

is looking at the Word of God and everything is fine with the soul.

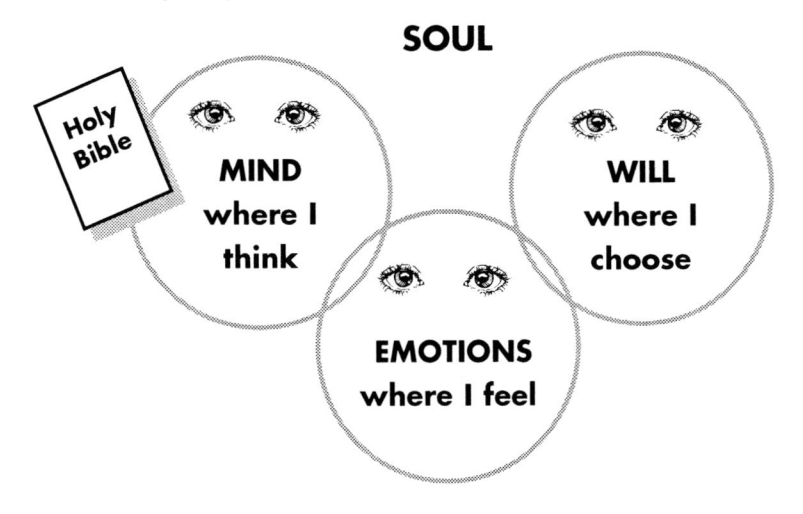

SOUL

MIND
where I think

WILL
where I choose

EMOTIONS
where I feel

Can you think of some **good** things that your mind could be thinking about . . .

THIS SOUL IS:

thinking – 'I know someone who needs help.'

MIND

choosing – 'I will help them today.'

WILL

feeling – 'I am happy to go and help them.'

EMOTIONS

Could you put the faces on this soul?

If a child had been horrible to you, and then you saw that child crying, what would you do?

I would..

What would this soul do if it saw a child hurt and crying, **even if this child had been really horrible?** _____

_____

_____

That child is hurt

MIND

I will help

WILL

I am sad that they are hurt

EMOTIONS

23

The soul could sing **Isaiah 61:10.**

Fill in the gaps.

I delight greatly in the Lord;

my _ _ _ _

_ _ _ _ _ _ _ _

in my God.

We need our minds to be 'renewed' as it says in Romans 12:2.

'Renewed' means 'made new'

If you find yourself thinking things that you know are wrong, ask Jesus to help make your mind new.

Then you will think like Jesus.

Memory Verse

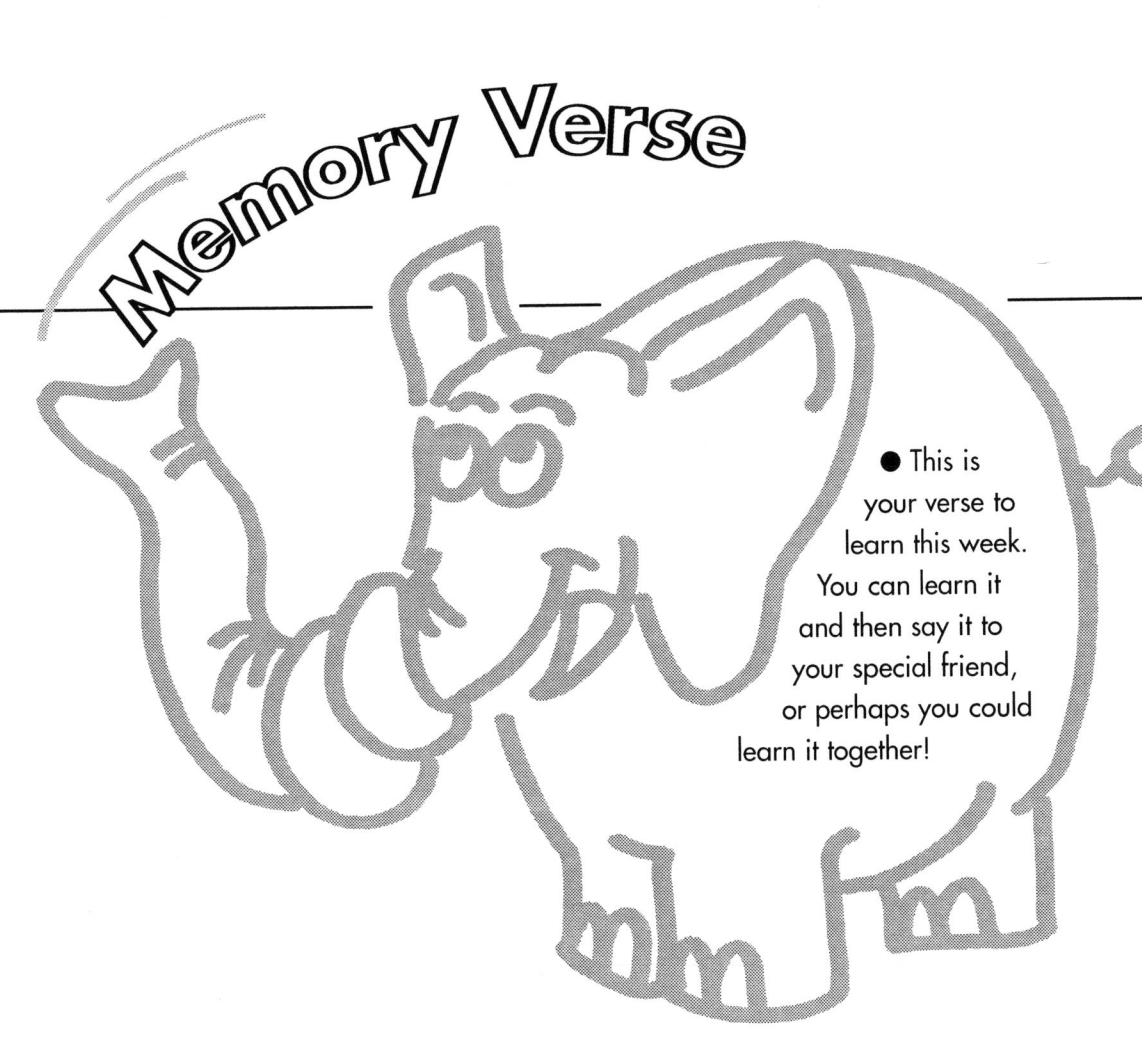

● This is your verse to learn this week. You can learn it and then say it to your special friend, or perhaps you could learn it together!

I delight greatly
in the Lord;
my soul rejoices in
my God.

Isaiah 61:10

25

More sharing together

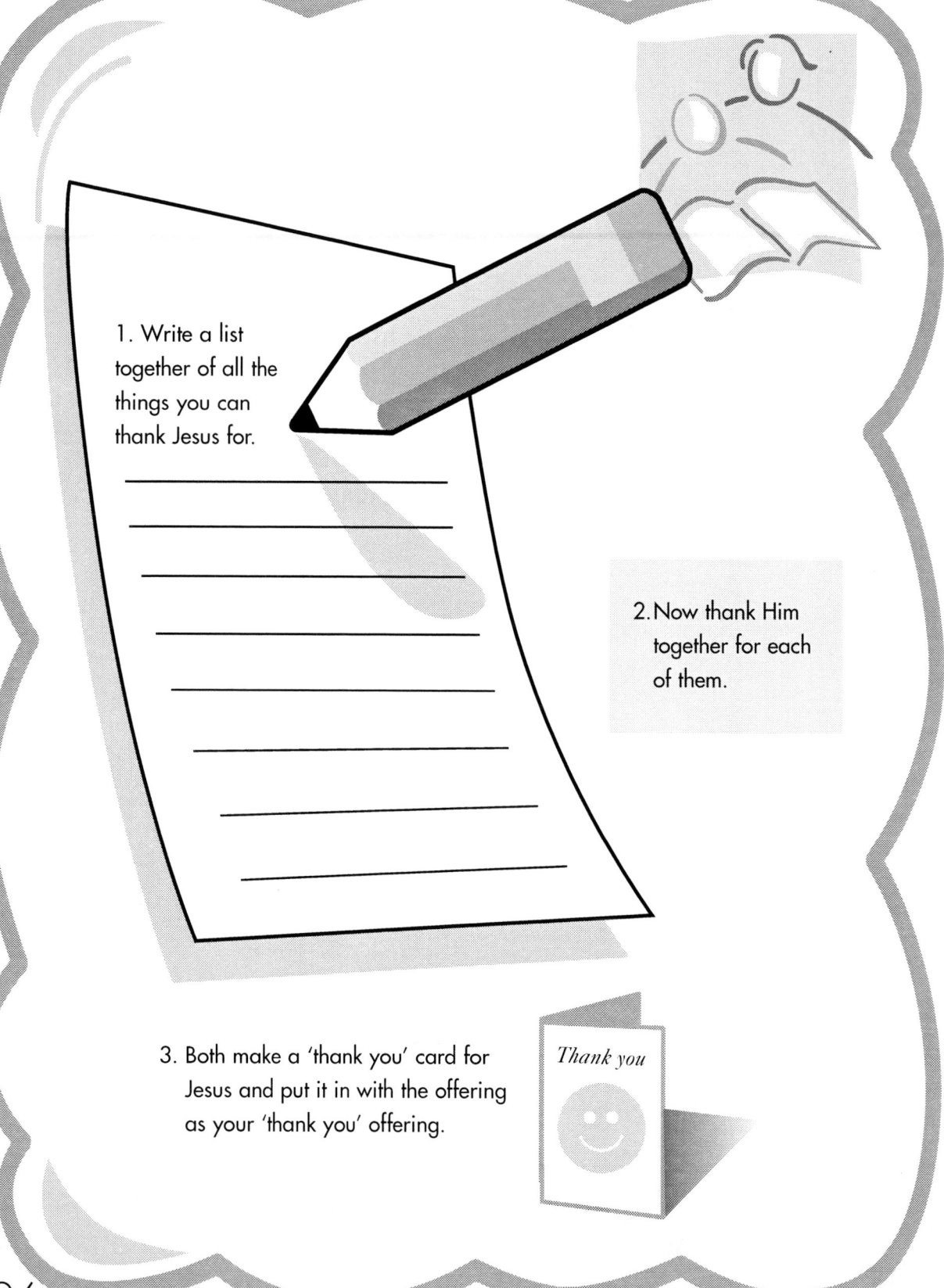

1. Write a list together of all the things you can thank Jesus for.

_____
_____
_____
_____
_____
_____
_____
_____

2. Now thank Him together for each of them.

3. Both make a 'thank you' card for Jesus and put it in with the offering as your 'thank you' offering.

Thank you

4

The enemy

The enemy

Today the enemy has entered the soul!

The enemy is from Satan's kingdom – what is the enemy?

Look back at Session 2 and write the names of the enemy from Satan's kingdom. I have done one for you.

Using money wrongly

Sometimes they hold on strongly – it is so hard to stop doing these things.

They are

STRONGHOLDS

What happens to the soul that has strongholds?

STEALING

Thoughts

Will to choose

Feelings and emotions

The soul says . . .

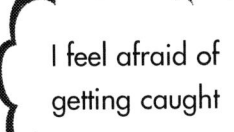

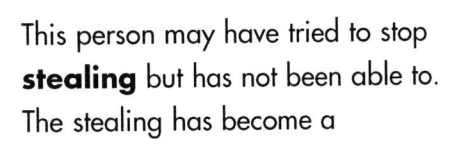

I want that toy

MIND

I will take it

WILL

I feel afraid of getting caught

EMOTIONS

This person may have tried to stop **stealing** but has not been able to. The stealing has become a

stronghold.

The soul is in trouble because **strongholds are from Satan's kingdom of darkness.**

The soul needs to cry out in the words of
Psalm 38:22

Come _ _ _ _ _ _ _ to help me,
O Lord my
S _ v _ o _ r.

SOUL

Thoughts **Will to choose**

STEALING

Feelings and emotions

Memory Verse

● This is your verse to learn this week. You can learn it and then say it to your special friend, or perhaps you could learn it together!

My help comes from
the Lord,
the Maker of heaven
and earth.

Psalm 121:2

More sharing together

1. Ask your special friend about a time when they asked Jesus to help them.

2. Say the rap (page 16) together a few times. You could use some percussion instruments, made from things in the house (check it is all right to use them first) as you say it together.

5

Down with strongholds!

Down with strongholds

'Come quickly to me, O Lord my Saviour.'

I need help to stop stealing. It has become a stronghold!

SOUL

Thoughts

Will to choose

Feelings and emotions

STEALING

This soul has asked for help!

Q Who is greater, Satan who controls the stronghold, or Jesus?

_____

Yes, but first the soul must decide that it wants the stronghold to go.

I want to stop stealing

I will stop stealing

I feel upset about stealing

MIND

WILL

EMOTIONS

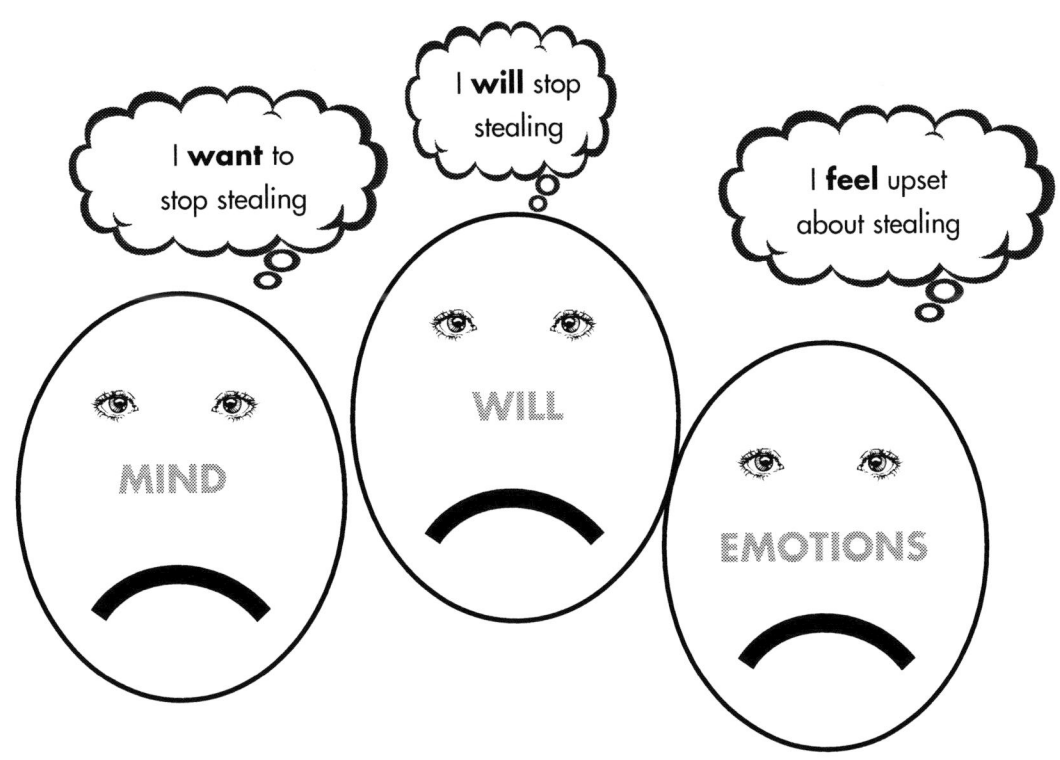

This is called '**repentance**' or being really sorry.

Every **stronghold** is sin, and the soul needs to repent, or be sorry, for sin.

Now **Jesus** can come with the **power of His Holy Spirit.**

The one who is in _ _ _ is _ _ _ _ _ _ _ than the one who is in the world. 1 John 4:4b

The stronghold must then go

GO! →

Stronghold (stealing)

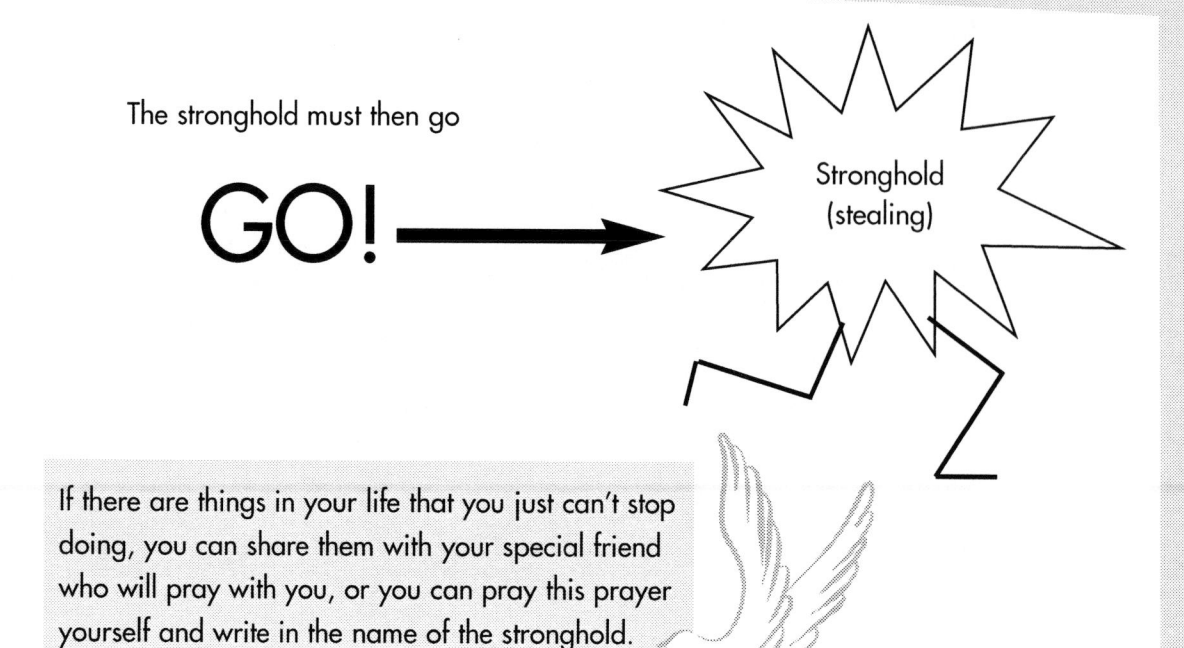

If there are things in your life that you just can't stop doing, you can share them with your special friend who will pray with you, or you can pray this prayer yourself and write in the name of the stronghold.

Lord Jesus,

    I find that I keep on _____.

I just can't stop by myself. I am really sorry that I do this time after time and I want to stop it.

    I know that you are greater than this. I now ask that by the power of your Holy Spirit you drive this stronghold out of my life.

    Thank you for doing this for me.

              Amen

Memory Verse

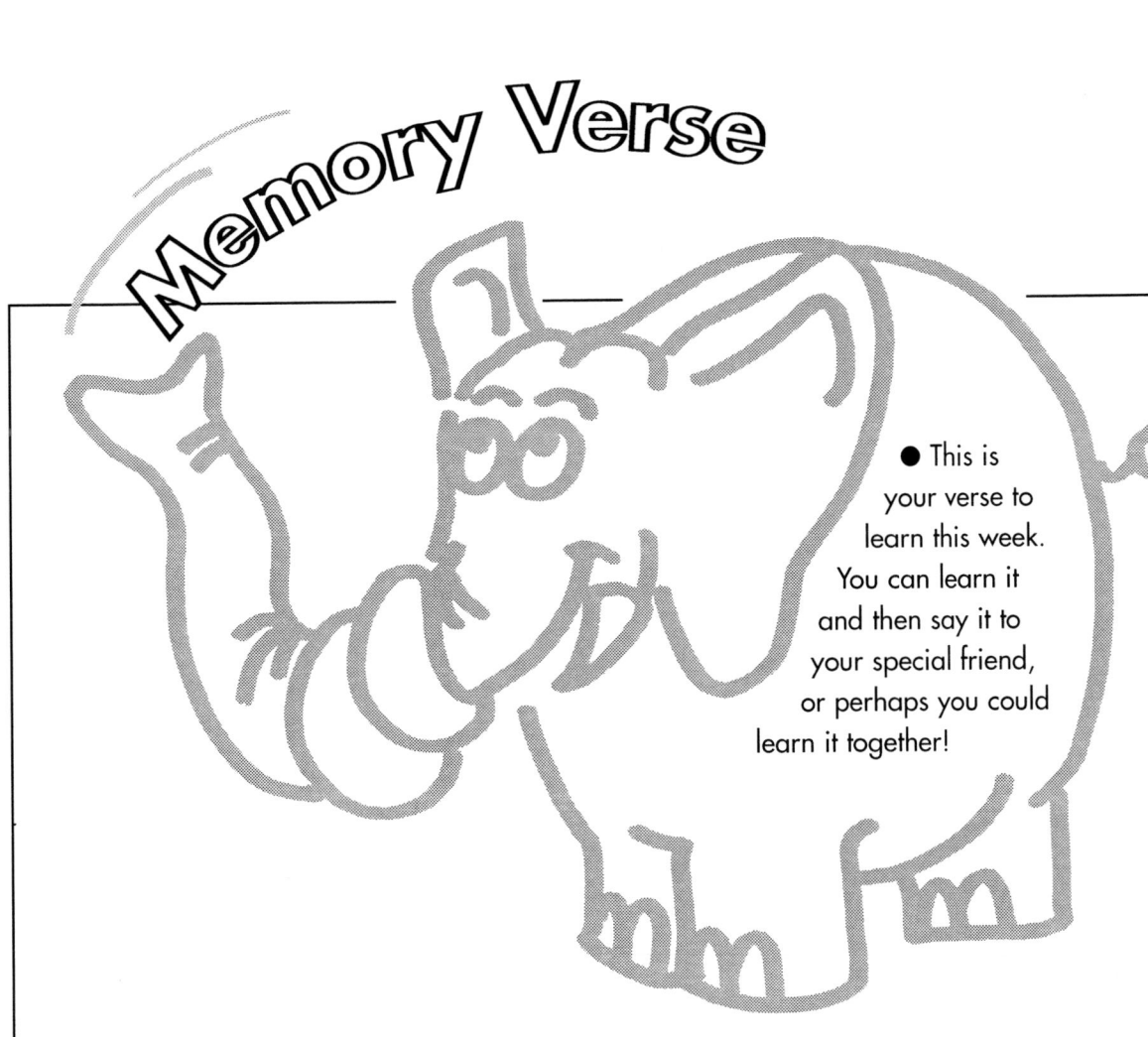

● This is your verse to learn this week. You can learn it and then say it to your special friend, or perhaps you could learn it together!

The One
who is in you
is greater than the one
who is in the world.

1 John 1:4

More sharing together

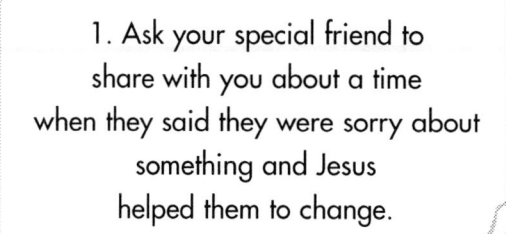

1. Ask your special friend to share with you about a time when they said they were sorry about something and Jesus helped them to change.

2. Say the rap (page 16) together again.

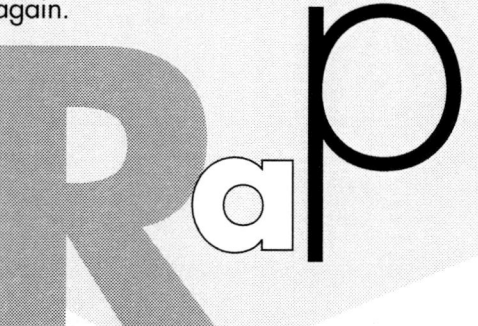

Rap

6

Looking back and going on

Looking back and going on

Do you remember talking about the soul and strongholds?

You prayed about something that had a stronghold in your life.

What was it?

I would like to know how you are getting on.
Tick one of these:

☐ I still have trouble from time to time.

☐ I am free – and don't do it any more.

☐ I still have lots of trouble and need some help.

Now I am going to draw some pictures and let you put the words in – what do you think they are saying?

40

Remember – every stronghold is weaker than Jesus!

Memory Verse

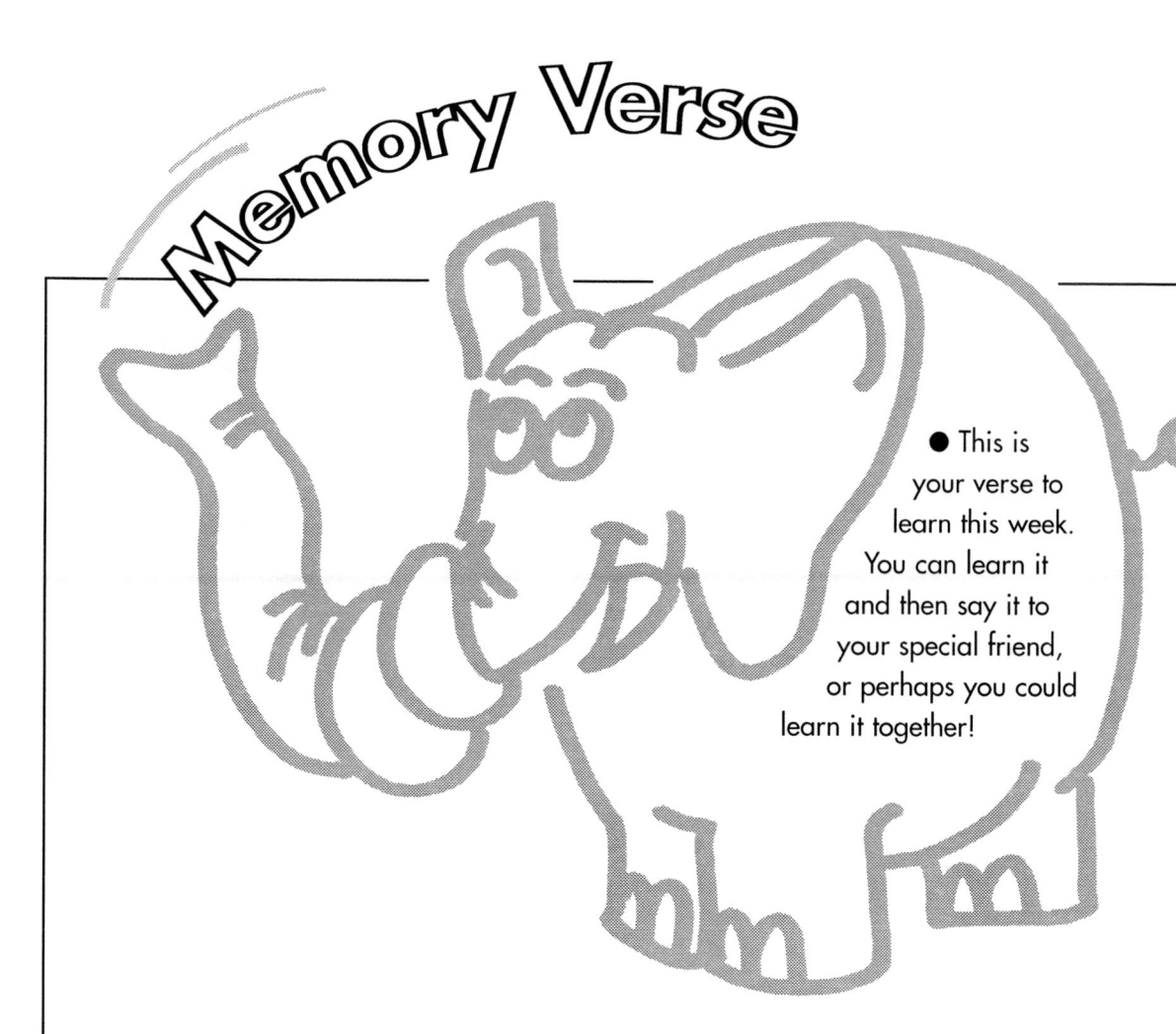

● This is your verse to learn this week. You can learn it and then say it to your special friend, or perhaps you could learn it together!

We take captive
every thought to make it
obedient to Christ.

2 Corinthians 10:5

More sharing together

1. Make a stronghold cartoon together.

2. Together teach someone the rap on page 16.

43

Both of you, please write your favourite verse from this book here

If you have any questions from this book, write them here to ask your special friend.

_____

_____

_____

_____

_____

_____

_____

_____

_____

_____